CURTIS INTERNATIONAL
PORTRAITS OF GREATNESS

General Editor
Dr. Enzo Orlandi

Text by
Agostino Ghilardi

Translator
Salvator Attanasio

Published by
ARNOLDO MONDADORI EDITORE
and
THE CURTIS PUBLISHING COMPANY

THE LIFE & TIMES OF ST. FRANCIS

CURTIS BOOKS
A division of
The Curtis Publishing Company
Philadelphia • New York

The first of the series of frescoes painted by Benozzo Gozzoli in 1452 was inspired by the legend, widespread in the 15th century, that Francis, like Jesus, was born in a stable between an ox and a little donkey. This tradition holds that the oratory of St. Francis in Assisi (*photograph on right*) was the saint's birthplace. A Latin inscription in Gothic script on the stone arch reads: "This oratory was the stable of the ox and of the donkey where Francis, mirror of the world, was born." The inscription dates from the fourteenth century.

On the adjoining page (5): a street in Assisi with the belfry of San Rufino. The church, begun in 1140, was completed in 1228, the year in which Gregory IX consecrated its altar. The interior contains the ancient font where Francis, Clare and perhaps also Frederick II (1197) were baptized by immersion.

"FRANCESCO" LIKE THE WOOLEN CLOTH OF FRANCE

A male child was born in Assisi in 1182 to Pietro Bernardone, a successful wool merchant, and his wife Pica, a native of Provence, whom Pietro had met on one of his many business trips to France. At the time of the child's birth in the big and comfortable house near the marketplace where the ancient Roman temple of Minerva still stands, the father was far away from home; he was busy buying uncut French woolen cloth in the marketplaces of Champaigne, Troyes and Montpellier, to which the wool-makers of Assisi usually brought their finished products.

When Pica brought her new-born infant to the church to be baptized, she decided to call him Giovanni, or John. But when Pietro returned from his journey, he insisted that his son be given another name. It was to be something that was really new and fashionable, a name that had the ring of richness: Francesco, or Francis, like the warm and precious woolen cloth of France.

The first biographers of Francis of Assisi called their writings *legends*, and in a certain sense the story of his life is legendary, so much so that one tends to doubt whether the hero really lived. But by using these legends, chronicles and documents as guideposts, we can reconstruct with historical accuracy the human adventure of the *Poverello*, the Poor Man of Assisi.

With a businessman for a father, Francis was at first more concerned with business matters than with learning. At that time, scant importance was attached to learning. In the episcopal school under the arcade of the church of St. George, the boys learned to read and write on the "board," a kind of primer composed in the main of prayers in the vernacular and psalms in Latin. The pupils were also taught some elements of grammar and rhetoric and perhaps some French which, being the language of trade, was fashionable. Francis did not particularly shine at school. Like his affluent fellow-students, sons of property-owners like himself, he was impatient to become part of the vigorous life of his time.

THE IMPERIAL GARRISON
IS SWEPT AWAY

The Assisi in which Francis grew up bristled with towers and belfries. It was enclosed within a ring of sturdy walls and dominated by the Rock which perched menacingly above the town.

At that time the master of the Rock was the formidable Corrado of Lützen, Duke of Spoleto. His position was a reward for faithful services to Henry VI, the Holy Roman Emperor. Corrado was a brutal and overbearing man. His eccentricity had earned him the nickname "fly in the brain." He had allied himself with the feudal lords against the Commune and the people, and in the process had managed to arouse such deep resentments among Assisians that two wholly disconnected events sufficed to bring his rule to a violent end. One was the sudden death of Henry VI, the other the elevation to the papal throne of Lotharius of Segni, who took the name of Innocent III. The new pope was a young, dynamic personality. He wanted to restore his sovereignty in Rome and in the territory that belonged to the popes, and he also claimed title to the Duchy of Spoleto, including Assisi. Thus Corrado was summoned to Narni where he handed over to Innocent III the lands which he had been holding in the name of the Emperor. In Assisi this was a signal for the smouldering resentments to burst into the flame of revolt: the angry populace wiped out the Imperial garrison along with the detested symbols of the ancient feudalism.

From old documents we can reconstruct Assisi as it was in the time of St. Francis. To get an accurate idea, however, we must reduce the present-day city by about one third, ruling out the lower part which runs in a straight line from the Basilica of St. Francis up to the Basilica of St. Clare.
Assisi had undergone a further development when it was painted, around 1490, by Nicolò da Foligno, called the Pupil, in the altar-piece reproduced above and dedicated to St. Rufino, patron of the city. This painting may be the oldest representation of Assisi as a medieval city, bristling with towers and belfries, enclosed
by high walls, and dominated by the Rock. The Rock of Assisi (left on adjoining page) rises on the ruins of the structure which was destroyed in 1198 in the rising against Corrado of Lützen. The construction of the new Rock was begun in 1367 by Cardinal Albornoz and completed under Piccinino (1458), Sixtus IV, and Paul III. The munificence of the popes is attested to by the coats-of-arms at the entrance to the structure. The ancient medieval castle was host to Barbarossa in 1160, and some ten years later, to his nephew, Frederick II.

THE DEFEAT AT COLLESTRADA

Inevitably the revolt of the Assisians spread from the Rock to the whole city. Many noblemen who had enjoyed privileges under Corrado were still hiding in and around Assisi. Now the populace vented its fury upon them. One by one the castles of Sassorosso, Montemoro, Poggio, Bassano came crashing down under the assaults of the knights and foot soldiers of the Commune of Assisi. The chronicles do not say whether Francis took part in these assaults. We may guess he did. He was only sixteen at that time but he was the son of a merchant whose vital interests were at stake.

What is certain is that three years later, in 1202, Francis fought with the Assisian cavalry against Perugia, the perennial rival city which had allied itself with the exiled noblemen of Assisi. The battle took place at Collestrada and the Assisians were badly defeated. Francis, along with other knights, was taken prisoner and thrown into jail in Perugia.

The suburbs of Assisi began outside the ancient belt of walls. Beyond them were the castles whose lords demanded tolls by authority of an imperial charter. These privileges restricted communal freedoms and slowed down and hampered trade. This was why the Companies of the Arts, the squads of communal archers and knights (depicted here in the triptych The Miracle of San Rufino *by Nicoló de Foligno) rose against them, burning their castles and driving out the feudal lords with the fury and impetuosity that was characteristic of the age.*

GOLDEN YEARS FOR THE MERCHANTS

In the new climate of communal freedoms, trade replaced "self-sufficient" production. Thus in Siena, as in Assisi, as shown by this detail of Lorenzetti's fresco which describes "the effects of good government in the city," the piazza, *or public square, became the center of all the trade and commerce of city life.*

After these stormy events, life returned to normal in Assisi. What had changed? Seemingly, very little. The peasants returned to their fields, the artisans to their shops, the man-servants and maid-servants to their usual chores. For many it had been merely a question of changing masters. The judges, notaries, some un-compromised noblemen, and the big merchants were now the rulers of the city, called the "majors" to distinguish them from the common people, the "minors." They sat in the courts dispensing justice next to the bishop, the prior of San Rufino or the papal emissaries. What had changed? The only change was that the many tiny, autonomous, independent communities which formerly had existed in the city and in the surrounding countryside, whose needs had been attended to by the feudal lord, now became the responsibility of the Commune, of the municipal administration. This gave rise to new problems. The defense of the city from enemies within and without its gates was no longer the task of the imperial garrison but that of the army of the Commune. This army had to be equipped with adequate weaponry. And the populace had to be supplied day in, day out with raw materials and food. These were two enormous maws to feed. Moreover, after the hardships and restrictions of the years of trouble the people no longer cared to put up patiently with misery and shortages. There was a thirst for luxury. People competed with each other in dress and in display. The merchants were the only ones who could satisfy these cravings.

Pietro Bernardone, the father of Francis, stood out among the merchants of Assisi. According to the chroniclers he was a very rich man. Like the other merchants he enjoyed the freedoms that the new age had granted to enterprising businessmen. He set up shop on the *piazza,* or public square, of Assisi where he displayed the precious fabrics from Normandy and Flanders: light silk-shot material, silk shawls, black and brilliant red velvets, heavy brocades, gauzes, camlets, precious satins.

From behind his counter, Francis studied the customers. He was so amiable and gracious that many preferred to deal with him rather than with the curt and authoritarian Pietro Bernardone.

The new middle class of Assisi, together with the artisans, was concentrated in the narrow medieval streets, some of which still remain (above), almost unchanged by time. Below: the Palace of the Consuls, seat of the communal magistrature, the custodian of the new freedoms.

KING OF
THE FEASTS

In the Assisi of that time privileged groups also led a kind of *dolce vita*. This pleasure-loving life was the product of the social strife and tensions of an age in which charity could exist next to ferocity, good breeding next to vulgarity, and love next to hate. Lorenzo the Magnificent was still in the wings of history but in 1200 there were already people in Assisi who lived by his maxim: Let him who will be glad follow his bent, for of tomorrow there is no certainty.

There were real companies of pleasure-loving persons, the *Societates Tripudantium*, with statutes and programs. Their only aim in life was to organize feasts and banquets, jousts and ceremonial processions. Francis, the son of Bernardone, could not remain apart from groups of this kind. He was a brilliant, refined youth, as openhanded as his father was miserly. Therefore he was always picked to be "the king of the feasts." This was a privilege extended to few, the only drawback being that the person so honored had to foot the bill.

Francis went from feast to feast, throwing money around "as though he were the son of a prince." But often at the end of these revelries he would suddenly experience a feeling of terrible inner emptiness.

In the fresco on the page to the
left, Lorenzetti illustrates
another aspect of the "effects
of good government": the joy in
living that dominated the city.
During the Spring bacchanals in
Assisi, "the damsels danced on
the squares, crowned with roses,
all luxuriously dressed, with
belts of gold and silver,
overgarments of velvet and
mantles of white silk thrown
sideways over their shoulders."
The fresco (right) by Gozzoli
shows a man of the people as
he spreads a cloak for Francis,
"the king of the feasts," to walk on.

THE AMBITION
TO BE
A KNIGHT

"A better name than knight cannot be found for a perfect man," asserts the Kleines Kaiserrecht (Abridged Imperial Law). St. Martin was a knight; the fresco on the left shows him receiving the investiture from Emperor Constantine. The work is by Simone Martini, who painted it around 1320 in the Lower Basilica of Assisi. In the beginning, knighthood was "an armed force at the service of unarmed truth." Born with religious ideals, it later degenerated into "the gay science," in a profession of adventure. St. Francis adopted its ideals, elevating its virtues. The illustrations reproduced here are taken from the poem "Eneit" by Heinrich von Veldeke (13th cent.) and from "Lancelot du Lac."

The "gilded youth" of thirteenth-century Assisi was no different from its modern counterpart in any medium-sized city. At a certain point boredom and weariness would set in. It was enough to climb as far as the ruins of the Rock and look beyond the city's walls to realize that the world did not end there, and that it might be worthwhile to try to escape from a monotonous round of pleasure.

Francis began to feel that need. Although very young, he realized that he could not continue forever to be the "king of the feasts." He had thought deeply during his year in the prison of Perugia, although, once liberated, he had once more dedicated himself to an exuberant enjoyment of life. The sudden onset of a serious illness forced him back into solitude. But it was not the solitude of the sickbed. It was something quite different. Francis was now aware of a deep inner solitude.

The greatest ambition of the adventurous youth of that time was to become a knight. Knighthood was at one and the same time a spiritual profession and a noble adventure. The Crusaders, the armed monks, and those nobles who fought for lofty ideals and for the honor and love of high-born ladies were all knights. To be a knight also meant being courteous and magnanimous. These were necessary qualities in a time when knighthood was not only a social status into which one was born, but was also open to aspirants from other selected social groups. Even merchants could become knights if they were able to show that they lived in a lordly manner. They could perform no manual work in the conduct of their affairs. In contrast to peddlers, they were required to sell cloth in whole pieces, wholesale and not retail. If they were iron merchants, they had to sell their iron by the ton and not by the ounce. Further, they had to keep a servant and a horse in the field, a luxury that only the very rich merchants could afford.

As a rich merchant's son, Francis also must have attempted to gain the collar of the order of knighthood. He had decided to leave Assisi and to become the groom of an Assisian nobleman who was off to the wars.

A MYSTERIOUS VOICE

Francis had equipped himself with all the necessary paraphernalia, a horse, weapons, and a rich and elegant uniform that was the admiration and envy of the other knights. All he had to do was to set out on his journey. Everything was ready for the expedition. But a singular event took place on the eve of his departure. An impoverished nobleman of Assisi could not join in the expedition because he was too poor to purchase the required suit of armor. Francis did not hesitate for an instant. In an impulse of generosity he stripped himself of his own and gave it to the poor nobleman. That very night he had a dream; for the first time he heard a sweet and mysterious voice that spoke to him. It seemed like a rewarding echo to his act of generosity. At any rate it was the beginning of a "dialogue" that was to continue and become increasingly urgent. The lives of many saints have been guided by this "voice." It always involves very singular and personal experiences and all we can do is to trust the contemporary accounts. "That night, while he was busying himself with last minute preparations and burning with a desire to leave, someone appeared to him who called him by name and led him into an enormous splendid palace, full of arms and knights, shining lances and shields and other weapons of war hanging on the wall. Francis looked about him in a state of joyous wonderment. He was not used to seeing such weapons and escutcheons in his house where he was more likely to see heaps of woolen cloth to be sold. In his wonderment over the happening he asked out loud who it was that owned these marvelous weapons and the splendid palace. The same voice replied that these things belonged to him and his knights. Thereupon Francis awakened in a happy state of mind. He interpreted the vision as an omen of a great future, and set out for Apulia . . ."

He galloped for a whole day and arrived at Spoleto. He was tired and felt a strange sense of uneasiness. No sooner did he close his eyes than the voice, mysterious, distant, yet clear as though it came from within himself, again addressed him: "Francis, who can do more for you, the Lord or the Servant?" "The Lord," he answered. And the voice said: "Therefore why do you leave the Lord for the servant, and the Prince for the vassal?" "O Lord, what do you wish me to do?" asked Francis humbly. "Return to Assisi and what you are to do will be revealed to you there."

Left: the dream of Francis depicted by Gozzoli in the Montefalco cycle: a majestic palace adorned with escutcheons and arms with the signs of the cross of Christ. The biographers add that Francis also glimpsed a marvelous woman waiting for her bridegroom. From this he drew the augury that, after becoming a knight, he would conquer everything that was shown to him in the dream.

Two episodes in the conversion of Francis: (right) the gift of his cloak to a poor man, a detail from Gozzoli's fresco; (above), Francis kissing the leper, as depicted in an 18th-century print in the Museum of the Capuchins in Rome. The latter episode played a crucial role in the Saint's life. He himself explicitly recalled it in his famous Testament.

"GO, FRANCIS, AND REPAIR MY HOUSE"

Francis returned to Assisi. He knew that this would arouse his father's ire and the criticism of his fellow-citizens. But the voice had talked to him in a way that excluded even the idea of disobedience. Now he went looking for solitary places so that he might again hear the voice which was to point out his way to him.

"One day while passing in front of the church of St. Damian, he felt an irresistible urge to go inside. He prostrated himself before the image of Christ with devotion, supplicating Him. Suddenly he felt like a completely different being. While he was in the grip of this emotion, the image of Christ crucified—an unheard-of prodigy in the course of centuries—began to talk with its painted lips. He called him by name and said to him: 'Go, Francis, and repair my house because it is falling into ruin.' Francis was stupefied. He trembled all over and almost went out of his mind at those words. He prepared himself to obey and summoned all his energies in order to carry out the command."

The tiny church of St. Damian as it is (photographs on adjoining page) and as it was transfigured by Giotto in his frescoes of Assisi. As can be seen on left, Giotto imaginatively reconstructed it in order to paint St. Francis inside it in the act of listening to the Crucifix. Center: the miraculous Crucifix whose lips moved. On the adjoining page: two views of St. Damian revealing its characteristic simplicity. Looking at it from the outside one can see that originally it must have been of even more modest proportions, composed of two parts, the forward part of which was added later.

For about a month Francis escaped his father's wrath in a hideout in the dwelling of the chaplain of St. Damian. The scene is depicted with a touching naiveté in a miniature of the 15th century (reproduced on the adjoining page) taken from a codex called Franchesina. *The ecclesiastical court which heard the case* against Francis presumably met in the open, as Benozzo Gozzoli shows in his fresco. The sentence was handed down in the tiny square between the bishopric and Santa Maria Maggiore, which was Assisi's main church. The trial drew a large crowd, interested in the affairs of two persons who were so well known in the city.

THE
GREAT STEP

A radical change had come over Francis, which greatly troubled his father. He could not understand why his son, once so merry, was now so quiet and introspective. Francis now spent his days in the little rustic church in which stood the Crucifix that had addressed him. The dialogue continued in the silence of the tiny temple: "If you want to fulfill my will, Francis, you must scorn and abhor all that which you have desired and loved up to now, according to the flesh."

Francis instantly obeyed. He began to strip himself of all his possessions and gave them to the poor. But the voice had also commanded him to rebuild the church. This required money. So Francis took a roll of scarlet cloth from his father's shop, mounted a horse and galloped to Foligno. There he sold the roll and the horse and returned to Assisi. The old priest of St. Damian, aware of the youth's eccentricities and Bernardone's temper, refused to take the money. Francis then left the purse on a window sill and asked the priest if he could remain in the service of the church. Now of full age, he could do what he pleased. Thus he performed the first act of his religious life: he became an "oblate" and thereby came under ecclesiastical jurisdiction.

Bernardone's reaction was swift: he demanded the return of his son and the money. Francis tried to escape by hiding. In spite of Pica's protests, Bernardone carried things to an extreme. He demanded that his son make public amends, that he renounce all hereditary rights, and that he be banished from the Commune in accordance with the law. Francis was summoned to appear before the consuls but he refused on the grounds that he was now a religious. Bernardone then took his case to the episcopal court before which Francis was legally bound to make an appearance.

In October 1206, father and son met before the court in the tiny plaza in front of the bishopric. Bernardone repeated the charges in an irate voice. Francis made no reply. Instead he stripped himself of his clothes with a decisive gesture and threw them at his father's feet. This was the great step—at 25 years of age he was now as poor as the Crucifix of St. Damian. Thereupon Bishop Guido rose from his chair, walked over to Francis, embraced him and then covered the youth's nakedness with his mantle.

FRANCIS BECOMES GOD'S BRICKLAYER

Francis took to the open road, not with Bishop Guido's mantle but with a tattered religious habit with a huge cross in chalk drawn upon it. Then, in the grip of a spiritual exaltation, he set forth singing praises to the Lord in sweet Provençal, the language of the troubadours. He began to wander through the countryside until he reached the territory of Gubbio. He was immensely happy but it was a happiness that was so personal that for the moment it could not be shared with others. He roamed through the woods, meditated in caves, and performed acts of penance. He lived as a hermit for about a year. He knocked on the doors of convents, offered to perform the meanest chores, begging alms from house to house. Then he decided to return to Assisi because the voice had summoned him to go back there. Thus the former elegantly dressed "king of the feasts" returned to his native city dressed in rags. His old friends hooted derisively at him, women made fun of him as he walked the narrow streets begging for lime and stones with which to repair the church of St. Damian. He had become God's bricklayer.

We know the names of numerous churches and chapels existing at the time of St. Francis. At least fifteen have been clearly identified. Some were under the jurisdiction of the bishop, others under that of the Canons of San Rufino, others under that of the Benedictines. Assisi was divided among these three religious authorities who were often rivals. The Benedictines played an important role in the life of the city and the countryside. They were responsible for the reclamation of the swamps of Chiagio, and for the irrigation of the plain. The photograph on left shows the interior of the church of the *Monastery of St. Benedict on the slopes of Mount Subasio where Francis spent whole days in prayer immediately after his conversion. Above, right: the tiny church of Porziuncola. It also belonged to the Benedictines but was given to Francis and became the cradle of the Order of the Friars Minor. A grandiose temple, whose construction took more than 100 years, from 1569 to 1679, has risen around the chapel. Francis settled in Porziuncola after his period as a hermit. The portrait on the adjoining page, by an unknown painter of the 15th-century Tuscan school, depicts him in this period of mystical exaltation.*

THE FIRST FOLLOWERS

Assisi is a city of churches. Even today there are twelve churches on a single street, the one that leads from the Basilica of St. Francis to the Piazza of Minerva.

If God's "bricklayer" had been enjoined to make repairs on all the crumbling temples and chapels a whole lifetime would not have been enough. Nevertheless, for two years, in obedience to the command of the voice, he clung tenaciously to this work and restored first the church of St. Damian and then that of St. Peter. Finally, he turned his attention to Porziuncola, the tiny chapel on the plain dedicated to the Blessed Virgin, so-called because of the "little parcel" of ground that surrounded it. It was at morning Mass in this tiny chapel that Francis was struck by the words of that day's Gospel. At the end of the service, he asked for an explanation. "Thus Francis heard that the disciples of Christ must possess neither gold nor silver nor money, nor carry wallets or purse, nor a staff on the road. Nor must they have footwear, nor two tunics, but preach only the kingdom of God and repentance. He was instantly gripped with divine fervor, and said: 'This is what I want, this is what I ask, and this is what I yearn to do with all my heart.' And he threw away the few wretched things that he still possessed. Then with a great fervor of spirit and with joy in his soul, he began to preach penance to all with simple words, but edifying his hearers with the sublime impulses of his heart . . ."

Francis had received a revelation at Porziuncola. He was to build the Temple of God, to bring the message among men as Christ Himself had done. At the beginning Francis, like Christ, also had twelve followers: Bernard of Quintivale, Pietro Cattani, Giles, Sabbatino, Morico, John of Cappella, Philip the Long, John of San Costanzo, Barbaro, Bernardo, Angelo Tancredi of Rieti, Silvester. They were mostly well-to-do citizens—Angelo was a knight—and considered as "majors" whose only wish now was to change themselves into "minors."

The histories of Francis' first companions have been told in a series of paintings hanging in the church of Rivotorto, executed by the Assisian painter Cesare Sermei (1609–1668). On adjoining page, left: the knight Angelo di Tancredi receives the religious habit from Francis. Below: the first twelve followers of Francis against the background of Assisi, from a miniature of the Franceschina codex. Right: the breviary used by Francis, written by Friar Leo. The open page contains the words of the Gospel which inspired his mission.

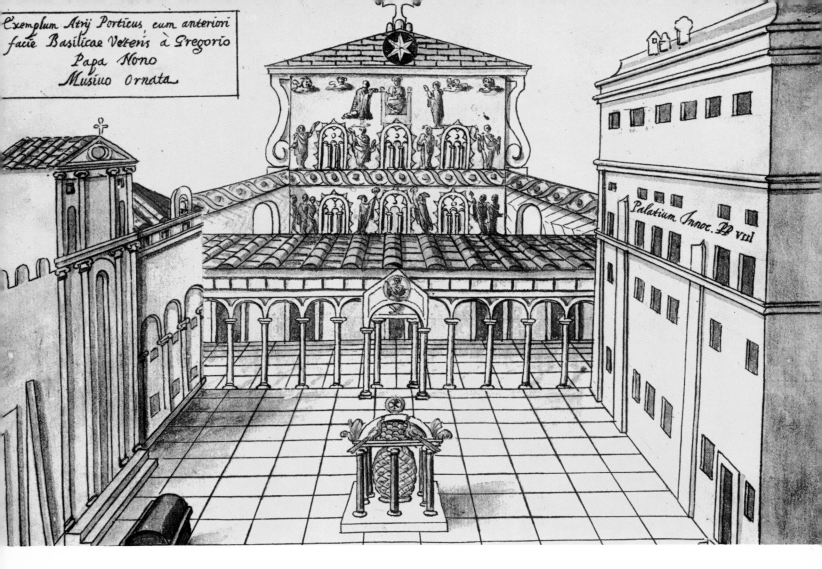

Palatium Innoc. PP VIII

HERESY
AND REPRESSION

Francis had never intended, at least in the beginning, to create a movement or to found a religious order. His only desire was to live according to the rule of the Gospel. His first companions had joined him because they had been attracted by his example.

The thirteenth century was rife with confraternities, sects, and even heresies. The conscience of the age was rebelling against the irreligious conduct of feudal bishops, the armed monks, and the spreading laxity in the monasteries. Unfortunately, it often happened that the reformers ended up in open rebellion and heresy. Whole communities, whole populations cut themselves off from Rome. From his chair, Pope Innocent III had repeatedly denounced the laxity of the clergy and, as a

man of action, had also launched a program of reform.

The dominant idea of the age was that the power exercised by the Church should prevail over temporal power, inasmuch as the flesh is subordinate to the spirit. This was the principle on which Innocent III based his activity as a reformer. He had the loftiest concept of papal authority and he was determined that spiritual power should be a reality. He had repeatedly taken steps against the Cathars, the Waldensians, the Humiliated and all the other sects which grew up overnight. They posed a threat to the Church with their concepts of poverty and their demand that a return be made to primitive Christianity. But the repression had been more harmful than the heresies themselves.

Francis went to Rome for the first time in 1206, immediately after his conversion. He did not wear the pilgrim's habit (a tunic with a large collar covering shoulders and chest, called the pellegrina) and he did not carry the staff from which the haversack was hung. He was dressed like a knight but—as his first biographers wrote—"for the love of poverty, he laid down his elegant robes and covered with ashes he sat in the vestibule of St. Peter among the beggars who abound in that place, considering himself one of them." Left: the atrium and the Basilica of St. Peter as they were in the years immediately following the Saint's death. Francis returned to Rome four years after his first journey, in 1210. Now he wore the uniform of poverty and had his first companions with him. Pope Innocent III received Francis and his followers in the Lateran (below, in an ancient print by Falda). In the Middle Ages it was the residence of the popes and for a long time had primacy over the Vatican Basilica itself. Right: the chair of St. Silvester in St. John in the Lateran. It was on this chair that the medieval pontiffs sat.

S IOANNES LATERA NENSIS TEMP° ANNI II∞

THE POPE'S DREAM

Above: the fresco by Benozzo Gozzoli which depicts the dream of Innocent III. The Pope saw Francis propping up the crumbling church. Right: the approval of the Rule in another fresco by Gozzoli. On the adjoining page, Pietro Valdo, one of the most noted heretics of the time, from an 18th century print. A rich merchant of Lyons, he founded, in 1170, the movement of the Poor of Lyons, also called the Waldensians. Precisely in 1210, the year in which Francis was in Rome to request and obtain papal sanction of the Rule, an eye-witness, the monk Burcardo, wrote in his Chronicon: ... "In those days we saw some of those who called themselves the Poor of Lyons, come to present themselves to the Holy See with a certain teacher of theirs, Bernard, in order to obtain sanctions and privileges ..."

At an audience in the spring of 1210 Pope Innocent III must have been startled when he was approached by a group of barefooted men who called themselves "The Penitents of Assisi," dressed in the coarse tunic worn by Umbrian peasants. The group was led by a young man, "short, thin, with burning eyes," whose face bore the marks of penitential self-denial. The presentations were made by Bishop Guido of Assisi. The thin man with the burning eyes began to speak: he did not protest against anybody or anything. He asked only to be allowed to live in evangelical poverty, according to the Rule that he had presented "written with few words, and making use above all of the texts of the Gospel."

Francis was petitioning for papal sanction for himself and his companions. Although Innocent III was disposed to encourage such movements and although he had approved other forms of penitential life during the twelve years of his pontificate—the Poor Catholics of Durando, the Poor Lombards of Bernardo—he was fundamentally a cautious soul. But he sensed something extraordinary in Francis's simple and passionate utterances and, unexpectedly, he adopted a special procedure. He verbally approved the Rule that Francis had presented to him. But, as the biographers report, the Curia put up a stiff resistance and everything would have gone at a much slower bureaucratic pace if two incidents had not crucially affected the Pope's decision: the intervention of Cardinal Giovanni di San Paolo and a dream which the Pope had that night. In his dream the Pope had seen the Lateran Basilica totter on its foundations and a poor man run to prop it up with his shoulders. He recognized this man as being Francis of Assisi. To Innocent the cardinal said this: "If we reject the petition of this poor man with the excuse that the Rule is new and too austere when he petitions us to approve a form of life that is in keeping with the Gospel, we must fear that we may displease the very Gospel of Christ." Thus was born the Franciscan Order.

In connection with the followers of Valdo (above) and Francis, Burcardo's account continues as follows: "The Holy Father noted certain of their superstitious practices: they removed the cover of their shoes in order to show that they went barefoot, they wore certain capes almost religious in appearance while they fixed their hair in the manner of lay persons; they were not ashamed to go together, men and women, and to live together under the same roof, and at times to sleep in the same bed, asserting that all this had been practiced by the Apostles. On the contrary, the Pope, instead of them, sanctioned others who called themselves Pauperes Minores *and who rejected such shameful practices, walked truly in bare feet in summer and winter, and did not accept money or any other thing . . ."*

SYMBOLIC RENT

Many flocked to hear him. One day a certain man from the Mark of Ancona humbly asked for admission into the Order. Francis told him: "If you wish to join the Poor of God first give your possessions to the poor of the world." The man left but, moved by love of kin, he divided his property among his relatives, leaving nothing for the poor. Upon returning to tell Francis about his generosity, Francis twitted him gently and enjoined him: "Begone, Friar Fly, because you have not yet emerged from your house and your kinfolk. You have given your possessions to your kinsmen and cheated the poor."

Francis did not ask an apparent poverty of his followers, but for a real renunciation of the goods of this world. He demanded an absolute evangelical poverty. The poverty of the other religious orders was different from that of the Franciscans. While the novice renounced his personal possessions, the order did not. It could accept any kind of property in money or lands. As a result abbeys and monasteries gradually extended their dominions and became large landowners. Franciscan poverty, on the other hand, was a new concept. Francis required that the friars possess but one tunic. They could not own books (very expensive then), nor could they travel on horseback because that was the mode of travel of the rich. Nor were they allowed to enjoy the comfort of a house of their own. He constantly reminded them: "The foxes have their lairs, the birds of the air their nests, but the Son of Man has nowhere to rest his head." Therefore he called the habitations of the friars *loca*, places and not convents. They were to be considered merely as stop-overs, places of transit. And in his Testament he left in writing that "all the houses of the friars must be built of wood and mud and that even the church should look poor." Thus poverty was extended from individual persons to the whole order. The tiny church of Porziuncola, which became the cradle and center of the order, never belonged to the friars. It always remained the property of the abbot of Mount Subasio. Every year the Poverello and his companions presented him with a basket of fish as symbolic rent.

"The first friars and those who for a long time came after them (in the miniature on the adjoining page) mortified their bodies beyond measure. They not only abstained from eating and drinking but also kept long vigils and endured bitter cold and performed excessive manual labor. They wore the harshest hair shirts and iron rings they could find on their flesh, hiding them from view." Thus states the Legenda antiqua di Perugia. *It also tells how Francis, following the example of Our Lord, retired to the desert where he prayed and fasted for forty days and forty nights "and wished to have in this world neither house nor cell and did not tolerate that one be built for him."*

HIS WORDS DISSOLVED HATREDS

During one of his journeys, Francis arrived at Arezzo but he could not enter the town because the inhabitants were at war with each other. Remaining outside "he saw on the walls of the city a great multitude of demons who were making merry. Therefore he ordered Friar Silvester, who was with him, to go towards the town gate like a town-crier and drive off the demons in the name of God. The friar obeyed and as soon as the demons departed, peace was restored to the city." The fresco, by Benozzo Gozzoli (below), depicts the episode as handed down to us by St. Bonaventure. On the adjoining page: two prints from the Museum of the Capuchins in Rome showing friars separating duelists and healing the sick.

CIVITAS·ARETII

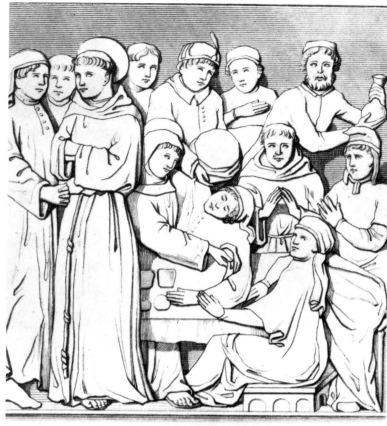

The Franciscan movement grew and attracted attention. Barely ten years had gone by and the twelve friars who had obtained papal sanction for their Rule now numbered three thousand. In a world in which "money had taken the place of God," this message proclaiming a rejection of earthly goods and possessions found a surprising response from those scandalized by a worldly Church. The humble friars, sent like a peaceful army to the four corners of the earth, acquired great importance in society and in the Church. They preached goodness and peace in cities divided by factional rivalries. But even more effective than their preaching was the greeting they addressed to every person they met, rich and poor, words which Francis had made obligatory: "May God give you peace!" These simple words stirred people to their depths, dissolving violent passions.

Francis had wanted his "minors" to be cut off from every earthly bond and to go through the world as messengers of peace. A friar who had accompanied Francis on his travels and who had heard him preach publicly recalled the following: "He very often preached the word of God before thousands and thousands of persons, and he was as poised as though he were conversing with one of his most intimate friends. A great multitude had the same effect on him as a single person,

and he preached to one man with as much solicitude as he would show towards a great throng. His purity of spirit gave him the necessary self-assurance to preach and he said marvelous things without preparation . . . But at times he was at a loss for words and at such moments he would give his blessing to the crowd, sending them away only with that but which never failed to make an impact on his listeners."

We have another testimony from Tommaso of Spalato, an archdeacon who was not a member of the Order. After listening to the Poverello preach in a public square in Bologna, on August 15, 1222, he wrote: "During the feast of the Assumption, I saw Francis preaching in the square in front of the Commune, where almost the entire population had gathered. His subject was: 'Angels, men, demons.' He spoke so well and with such perfection that this sermon, delivered by an illiterate, astonished very many educated personages present . . . The exclusive aim of all his utterances was to dissolve hatreds and restore peace. His tunic was torn and patched, his appearance pitiful, his countenance unbeautiful. But God endowed his words with such efficacy that many noble families, among whom the fury of ancient grudges had been unleashed in torrents of blood, became reconciled."

This detail from a 13th-century panel by the Maestro di Santa Chiara (left) shows Francis in the act of cutting the young girl's hair. Below: the silver urn preserving the blonde curls of the Saint. The relic is preserved in the Basilica of St. Clare.

The reaction of Clare's relatives is portrayed (right) in a detail of the same panel. Clare is determined to follow her chosen path to the end. Just before his death Francis sent to her and her companions his last instructions: "I, little Friar Francis, wish to follow the path and the poverty of our Most High Lord Jesus Christ . . . and I ask you, my ladies, and I counsel you, to live always in this most holy life and in this poverty." The humble dormitory of the Sisters that is still admired at St. Damian (left) clearly confirms that the Saint's will was respected.

for her in front of the church with lighted torches. Singing, they led her to the altar where Francis was waiting. She fell to her knees and consecrated herself to the Lord, vowing to follow Him in poverty according to the Rule of her teacher. She then removed her velvet gown and satin slippers and stripped herself of her jewels. In exchange, she dressed herself in a grey religious habit, tightened it around her waist with a string, and then slipped her feet into a pair of wooden clogs. Next, her blonde tresses were cut and dropped to the floor like scattered straws of gold. She did not deign to look at them but quickly covered her head with a black veil that was handed to her. As dawn was breaking, the group walked in solemn procession to the monastery of the Benedictine nuns, to whose care Francis had entrusted her.

Soon a violent knocking was heard on the door of the monastery. Men of arms belonging to the Offreducci clan had come to take her back. Clare hid in the church where no one could touch her without committing sacrilege, clinging to the altar. She could hear the threats, mixed with blandishments, of her armed kinsmen. She decided to go out and face them. She removed the veil and showed her shaven head. This was a sign that she would not turn back from her resolve. Astonished, the Offreducci fell back. Francis then realized that a safer asylum had to be found for Sister Clare. Together with Philip and Bernard, he accompanied her to another Benedictine monastery on Mount Subasio. Two weeks later Clare's sixteen-year-old sister, Agnes, came to join her.

St. Damian is one of the most spiritually impressive sites associated with the Franciscan order. It breathes the characteristic virtues of simplicity, humility, poverty and gladness. Clare and her sisters used to gather for prayer in the tiny choir (below) made of very humble stalls, disconnected benches, and a lectern supported by a squared log.

THE FORTRESS OF POVERTY

After having also consecrated Agnes to poverty, Francis requested the bishop of Assisi to lodge Clare, her sister and any other women who might want to follow their example in St. Damian. The prelate promptly gave his approval and the two young religious immediately settled in the place where the Crucifix had talked to their teacher.

They were not alone for long. Other girls, weary of the life of the time, made up their minds to wear the religious habit of poverty. After Agnes, Clare's other sister, Beatrice, and her mother, madonna Ortolana, responded to the call of the Gospel. Thus the illustrious family of the Offreducci was reestablished unexpectedly at the feet of the miraculous Crucifix. Clare's followers became so numerous—old friends of her childhood, close or distant relatives—that Francis called St. Damian the fortress of poverty. The church was as poor as the women who were lodged therein. Like the "minors," they took vows of poverty, chastity and gladness of spirit, and worked without recompense. They nursed lepers and often went hungry because, unlike the friars, they were forbidden to beg for alms.

"After the virgins of the Church had begun to gather in that place, and to achieve the height of perfection in the exercise of the loftiest poverty and in the splendor of all the virtues, the blessed father, little by little, deprived them of his corporeal presence, although he continued to take care of them. Once they had given numerous proofs of their supreme perfection and the Saint had assured himself that they were ready to endure all sacrifices and sufferings for the sake of Christ, he promised that he and his friars would always lend counsel and assistance to Clare and her sisters." But their admiration prevented St. Francis from going to St. Damian as often as he would have liked to. He wanted to be naught else but the humblest of creatures before God.

In 1219 Cardinal Ugolino drew up and approved a very strict Rule in which Clare, faithful to the teaching of Francis, insisted that the "privilege of poverty" be confirmed.

*According to tradition
St. Francis composed his
"Canticle to Brother Sun"
in this tiny convent which was
enlarged in the course of the
years without losing its
humble aspect (see the two
illustrations on this page).
"Living in a tiny cell of
mats, near St. Damian, sick,
and without seeing the light
of day for more than fifty
days, and moreover suffering
from great pains in his eyes
so that he could not sleep . . .
he wanted for his own comfort,
and for the edification
of his neighbor, to
compose a new hymn of
praise to the Lord,
talking about His creatures,
of whom we make use
every day and without whom
we cannot live."*

46

FIVE COURAGEOUS SOULS

It is almost impossible to reconstruct all the journeys made by Francis in Italy and abroad. For example, he certainly must have returned to Rome several times. An authoritative source describes his presence at the Fourth Lateran Council in 1215, during which the Poverello met St. Dominic, as shown in Gozzoli's fresco (below).

The friars were now a multitude. The seed that Francis had sown had yielded good fruit, and now he realized that the borders of Italy had become too narrow for the work of his followers. Thus he began to send them to other parts of the world, in small groups.

The first mission left for France, Germany, Hungary, Spain and the East. But they suffered many frustrations and disappointments according to the chronicles, particularly those written by Giordano da Giano and Thomas of Eccleston. One of the most disastrous missions was that to Germany, headed by John of Penna. "After entering that country the friars, who were completely ignorant of the language, when asked whether they wanted to be lodged and fed always answered *Ja.* Thus many people received them benevolently. Seeing that this word served to bring them good treatment, they decided to answer *Ja* to any question. Thus when they were asked whether they were heretics who had come to infect and pervert Germany, they unhesitatingly answered *Ja.* Some were beaten unmercifully, others imprisoned, while others were exposed to public mockery and pilloried." Their reception in Hungary was no better. ". . . The pastors unleashed dogs against the friars and without uttering a word, showered them with blows from their kitchen spits . . ." But the friars did not give up.

Five of them left Porziuncola to go to Morocco, passing through Alamquer, present-day Seville. Proclaiming themselves to be the ambassadors of the King of Kings, Jesus Christ, they were put into chains and dispatched to Morocco. Here, naked, "they intrepidly confessed and proclaimed their faith." They were cruelly yoked by their necks and dragged along the ground like sacks. The king promised to save their lives and provide them with money and women if they would convert to Islam. In reply, they proclaimed their contempt for all earthly things. So grabbing a sword the king himself beheaded them on the spot. When told of this, Francis exclaimed: "God be praised! Now I truly know I have five minor brothers!"

The miniaturist of the Franceschina *(above) shows us the friars who, following in the tracks of Francis, go on foot through the roads of the world with no other baggage save the yoke of obedience. Uppermost: Francis accepts lay persons, widows, and married couples into the Third Order. Those who joined pledged themselves to make peace with their enemies and to restore ill-gotten gains. Meanwhile, in the lands of the infidels, as the miniature on the adjoining page shows, the friars sealed their life with martyrdom.*

Here are several scenes, drawn by Doré, of the Crusade proclaimed at the time of Francis (from left to right and from top to bottom): Richard the Lion Hearted at the battle of Arsur; entry of the Crusaders into Constantinople; St. Francis before Melek-Kamel; massacre in the mosque of Cesarea; the sight of the Cross exalts the Crusaders; the profession of faith on the field of battle. Scorning the most elementary prudence, Francis, along with Friar Illuminato, appears before the Sultan. This meeting, depicted in a fresco by Gozzoli (adjoining page), kindled the imagination of his biographers to produce descriptions such as the ordeal by fire, clearly legendary.

THE INVINCIBLE WEAPON

Despite the failure of previous efforts, Innocent III insistently urged Christendom to a new Crusade. Hope lingered that the Holy Places in Jerusalem could be wrested from the infidels with a renewed fervor on the part of the faithful.

Francis was among those who responded to the Pope's appeal. Born to adventure, he embarked at Ancona with a few companions. After a month on the high seas he arrived at Acre and then Damietta, where the Crusaders were laying siege to the camp of Sultan Melek-Kamel.

One August day in 1219, the Crusaders saw a tiny, emaciated group, dressed in tatters, without shields, pickaxes or lances, approach their encampment. What did these ragamuffins want? This was immediately revealed by one of them, Francis, who spoke with utter simplicity and candor. They wanted to go over to the enemy lines and convert the Moslems. Giacomo da Vitry, the papal legate who happened to be in the Christian camp, saw Francis and his companions in person. He wrote the following from Damietta: "Their teacher who founded the Order came into our army encampment and, inflamed with zeal for the faith, he betook himself to the Saracen camp where for many days he preached the word of God to the infidels but with little success. But the Sultan, king of Egypt, asked him to beseech the Lord to let him know, through divine inspiration, which religion most pleased Him so that the Sultan might embrace it."

It was the first time that the Moslems of Melek-Kamel heard Jesus discussed by a Christian who came into their midst bearing only the weapon of faith. It must have been disconcerting, and if the Franciscan mission produced no brilliant results on the practical level, it certainly had a great significance from a spiritual point of view. The *Poverello* of Assisi, with an illuminating gesture, had made it clear that the Gospel is not to be imposed by force of arms.

OLDANV·MISIT·VNĀ·PVELLĀ·AD·TĒTĀDV·B·F·ET·IPE·ITRAVIT·IGNĒ·ET·OMNES·ESTVPVERVNT

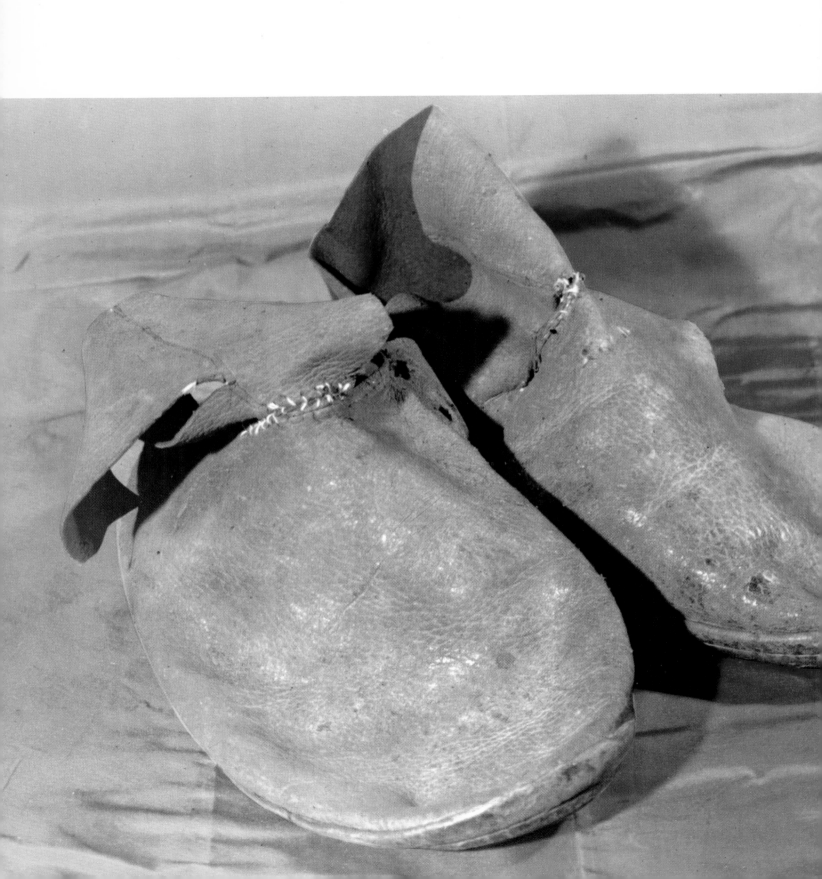

The most precious relics
of the Saint are preserved
in the sacristy of the
Basilica of St. Francis,
in a large wooden wardrobe
decorated with historical
legends. They consist
of small, humble, personal
things, preserved with loving
care by generations of
Franciscans. Among them
are: the tunic that the
Poverello wore in the last
days of his life and on which
there is a trace of the imprint
of the stigmata he bore;
the letter addressed to
Friar Leo; a ciborium
(vessel for holding the Host)
with several traces of blood;
finally the coarse gray tunic
habitually worn by the
Saint, and his sandals,
reproduced on these pages.
The history of each relic is
known, since the archives
of the Basilica contain
reliable testimony from 1338
to our day. According to
tradition, the tunic is
the same that Francis wore,
in obedience to the command
of the warden, when he was
on the point of death.
The story is told by his
first biographer, Friar
Tommaso da Celano. The
warden told him: "Put on
this tunic for holy obedience,
which I am merely lending
to you. And so that you may
be sure that you have no
property rights with regard
to it, I forbid you to
give it to others."

"THE LORD WILLED THAT I BE A MADMAN"

Great and bitter surprises were in store for Francis on his return from the Orient. Some friars, the very vicars whom he had appointed as deputies during his absence, had tried to introduce innovations into the Rule to temper the strictness of the vow of poverty. Some had gone even so far as to draw up a new Rule.

Informed in time by some faithful friars, Francis decided to return to Italy immediately. He made the return journey in a state of total weariness and exhaustion, plagued also by an eye disease contracted during his stay in Egypt. After arriving in Italy, "he did not go to those who had gone astray but directly to the Pope."

The Pope had approved the Rule and now Francis wanted the Pope to confirm it anew. He was certain that Honorius III, successor to Innocent III, would also defend his ideal and the Rule of life which now served as an inspiration to thousands of religious.

The new Pope appointed Cardinal Ugolino as protector of the Order. His task was to settle the many disputes that had arisen in the Order. Real factions had been created. On the one hand there were those who in time would be called the Spirituals and who championed absolute poverty; on the other the *Lassisti* who demanded a modification of the strictness of the Rule.

Cardinal Ugolino, the future Gregory IX, showed Francis the proper balance between the two forces. He made him understand that the heroic period that had been proper at the start now had to be followed by reflection and organization. Hence the Rule had to be modified somewhat. But at the "Chapter of the Mats" at which the "sage" friars seemed to prevail, Francis spoke as follows: "Brethren, God has called me to follow the voice of humility and He has pointed out to me the path of simplicity. I do not wish to hear any talk about any kind of Rule, either that of St. Augustine, or St. Bernard, or St. Benedict. The Lord has willed that I be a madman in the world, and God has not willed to lead us along any other path save this one."

The miniaturist of the Franceschina, *in the illustration above, dramatically depicts the temptations of money and of the comfortable life to which many friars were subject during the last years of Francis' life. Friar Elias (left) had been elected to preside over the Order; he belonged to the* Lassisti *or laxer tendency and is a much discussed personage. He advocated a strongly centralized organization. The "Spirituals" opposed him. Friar Elias was an energetic, enterprising man of achievement. This was seen during the construction of the Basilica of St. Francis in Assisi, which he wanted to build on a grandiose scale to honor the memory of his teacher. But later he ventured into another enterprise, that of reconciling the Church with the Empire, in an attempt to achieve the unity of Christendom. In this undertaking he was so utopian and incautious as to draw an excommunication from the Pope.*

nuta la volucre d ghicra ataccata   Decima quanto ala bstinentia

The first conflicts in the Order
broke out during Francis'
journey to the East and reached
their climax at the famous
Chapter of the Mats, portrayed in
an 18th-century print (above,
Museum of the Capuchins, Rome).
Upon his return to Italy Francis
realized that many brothers were
betraying their vow of poverty. A
new house had been built of stone
in Bologna. He avoided passing
through the city and ordered
his friars to quit the house
as quickly as possible. The
same happened in Porziuncola,
where, in his absence, the friars,
instead of the usual huts of twigs
and branches, had built a tiny
convent in brick. According
to ancient chroniclers:
"He climbed to the roof
and tore down the beams
and tiles with a decisive
hand." The miniature on
the adjoining page
shows the shelters of the
first Franciscans.

"LET POVERTY BE YOUR PARTY"

The last years of his life were embittered by continuous differences of opinion, degraded by polemical disputes. Francis, who aspired to live in solitude and in the mystical contemplation of God, found himself reluctantly involved in noisy conflict. The work that he had brought into being now had to be organized in accordance with the counsel of its cardinal-protector so that its continuity might be assured. This gave rise to endless and often fruitless debates. The first Rule, which had been drawn up simply and succinctly, using Gospel texts as guides, and which had been approved by Innocent III, no longer sufficed. New problems had arisen and in consequence the decisions adopted at the general chapter meetings now had to be incorporated into the constitution.

Francis wrote a new Rule with the aid of a learned friar of the Order, Cesario da Spira. It is the first one, not approved by a papal bull, that has been left to us. A second one, seemingly, was more or less intentionally lost by Friar Elias. Finally, Francis retired to Fonte Colombo to give a definitive form to the Rule. Here are some excerpts from it: "The Rule and life of the Friars Minor is this: observe the Holy Gospel of Our Lord Jesus Christ, living in obedience, possessing nothing of one's own, and in chastity. The friars who have promised obedience are to have only one tunic with cowl and, if they wish, another tunic without cowl. Those who are compelled by necessity may wear footgear. All friars are to be dressed in shabby clothes and they are to be patched with sackcloth or other rags, with the blessing of God. I invite and exhort them not to despise and judge men whom they see dressed in soft and precious garments and consuming dainty beverages and foods. Rather let each one judge and despise himself. I strictly forbid all the friars to receive monies in any manner, by themselves or through the medium of other persons. Only the ministers and the Custodians, thanks to spiritual friends, are to take care of such matters for the needs of the sick and in order to clothe the other friars.

"Friars are not to possess anything, neither house, nor lands, nor anything else whatsoever. They are to pass through this world as pilgrims and foreigners serving the Lord in poverty and humility and begging for alms with confidence and without shame. Let poverty be your party."

At the insistence of his friars, Francis retired to the hermitage of Fonte Colombo, on a ledge of the Rieti valley, in order to write the Rule. The photograph on the left shows us the Speco as it is today and as it must have been at the time of the Saint. Francis spent those days in prayer and solitude.

The first draft of the Rule turned out to be too long. Francis was distressed by the task of reducing what for him was the substance of life into a formula and articles. He wrote another that was more concise but it required Divine intervention to reassure the Saint, as the ancient miniature (below) shows us.

It fell to Honorius III, who succeeded Innocent III, to approve the Rule definitively. This happened on November 29, 1223, with the Bull Solet annuere. The papal sanction is represented (left) in the detail from the fresco by Giotto. The original of the Bull promulgated by Honorius (below) is in the Basilica of St. Francis.

55

THE FIRST CRIB

An altar has been erected on the boulder where Francis set up the first crib (below) and a sanctuary was established around the altar. If the name of the tiny town of Greccio in the Rieti valley is known throughout the world, it is almost exclusively due to the crib of the Poverello *of Assisi. Benozzo Gozzoli, in the fresco on the right, depicts*

Francis in the act of rocking the Holy Child. A doubt has risen among scholars of the Franciscan Order: was there a tiny statue depicting the Child in the crib fashioned by Francis? The first biographer seems to assert this, albeit implicitly.

Francis returned to the peace and quiet of Fonte Colombo at the beginning of the Christmas season in 1223. Freed from the agitations rocking the Order, his soul was absorbed in prayer and song. He wanted to celebrate a beautiful Christmas, a Christmas that would make him relive "the remembrance of the Child born in Bethlehem and see with the eyes of flesh the privations to which He was subjected, and how He was laid in the manger and how He rested between the ox and the little donkey." Thus the first crib was fashioned from a mystical and poetical impulse. The scene has been described in a simple, moving way by an eye-witness: "The day of gladness was drawing near. Friars, men, women, gathered from all parts; each one, with his or her soul full of joy, prepared candles and torches to illumine that night which was to illumine the centuries like a glittering star. The Saint of God finally arrived: he saw that everything had been prepared and was comforted. The manger was readied; it was stocked with hay and the ox and little donkey led into it. The night, as brilliant as day, was a delight to behold for men and beasts. The friars, with their canticles, rendered to God the praises that were due to Him. The Saint stood before the manger emitting deep sighs, gripped by devotion and in a transport of joy. The rite of the Mass was celebrated in the manger . . . and the Saint, who was a deacon, put on the vestments of the sacred function and sang the Gospel. His voice, passionate, sweet, clear, and sonorous, invited those present to consider the reward of heaven. He preached to the people on the nativity of the King who became poor and on the tiny village of Bethlehem, and he found words which were as sweet as honey. Often when he mentioned Jesus Christ, he burned with such ardor that he called Him the Child of Bethlehem and modulated his name like the bleating of a little lamb, the gentleness of his affection seemed to suffuse his mouth more than his voice."

It was so vivid that the crowd of worshippers really believed it was in Bethlehem. One of those present—according to the same account—"saw in the manger the Child who seemed emptied of life and the Saint of God advance towards Him in order to awaken Him from the torpor of sleep. It was a vision in keeping with reality because the Child Jesus had been forgotten in many hearts and with the help of Grace it was revived in these hearts by St. Francis."

THE PLACES OF SOLITUDE

Once the new Rule was proclaimed at the general chapter assembled in Porziuncola in the presence of the new vicar, Friar Elias, Francis increasingly cut himself off from the day-to-day concerns of the Order. He was tired, emaciated by his penitential practices, worn out by illness. He was only forty-two years old but he looked like a man who was finished. Even his activity can be said to have come to an end. It had covered a brief span of fourteen years: from the time of the approval of the Rule by Innocent III in 1210 to his retirement, in 1224, to the places of solitude. But how much work had been accomplished, how much joy had been experienced, how many battles had been fought, how much history had been written in these few years!

Now, feeling the approach of Sister Death, Francis sought the silences of those solitary places for which he had constantly yearned in the first years. Thus he retraced his steps along the old paths between the mountains and the forests, stopping once more in those caves which he had favored. Today these places are famous as Franciscan sanctuaries: the Carceri on the Mount of Assisi, Celle de Cortona, Speco di Narni, Satriano, Cetona, Chiusi, Greccio, Fonte Colomba, Poggio Bustone and La Foresta in the Rieti valley. To this day they have a powerful impact on the imagination of visitors. They have not changed very much since the time of the Saint. Even now these places contain many caves and grottoes, covered with deep woods, and broken by ravines and gorges. The grottoes were the actual dwellings of Francis and his first companions. Here, in the silence of these wild retreats, they prolonged their dialogue with God.

The miracle of water, painted by Giotto in Assisi, recalls an episode that occurred during the last climb to Mount Verna. Because of his infirmity the Saint rode a donkey guided by a mountaineer who was raging with thirst. Francis knelt to pray, and then he said to the thirsty man: "Go to that rock and you will find a spring." He did.

Above: the hermitage of the Carceri, on the mountain of Assisi. Francis retired there several times with his friars, who sheltered in the natural caves under the grove of ilex trees. He preferred steep and rocky places like the hermitage of Poggio Bustone (below), Mount Verna and others where nature was unspoiled.

"DON'T HARM THE FIRE"

Franciscan literature is full of the Saint's talks with animals and his preaching to the birds in particular. Painters could hardly be expected to neglect such a fascinating theme. Benozzo Gozzoli endowed his sermon to the birds with the aura of a fairy tale, in the manner of Beato Angelico, of whom he was a follower.

The two prints in the Museum of the Capuchins, in Rome, depict the greeting extended by the birds to Francis on the day he climbed Mount Verna (above), and the famous episode of the wolf of Gubbio who became tame in the presence of the Saint. Right (61): the idealized colloquy of the Poverello of Assisi with creation, executed by Schoor and Snyders.

"Listen to our brother birds who are praising the Lord; let us go among them and sing our canonical hours." Francis had just landed; it was the day of his return from the Orient. His heart was heavy but those chirpings amid the grasses and on the uppermost branches of the poplars on the tiny Venetian island on which he had landed had made him for a moment forget his tribulations. He turned to his companion and invited him to follow him. He wanted to see the creatures who with their song had dissolved his anguish. It was to be expected that the birds would fly away at the approach of the two friars: instead they remained hopping among the grasses, continuing their song with such fervor that Francis was forced to admonish them: "Brother birds, refrain from singing until we are finished with our prayers." The birds immediately grew quiet and resumed their singing with a new verve only after the two friars finished reciting their prayers.

Francis was the first to perceive what recent studies have shown, that creatures communicate with each other. He also perceived that there was a mode of communication between men and animals. There had to be a subtle bond between them inasmuch as they were all creatures of God.

Francis treated all animals as equals, whether he was addressing a rabbit, or a cicada, or a turtle-dove, or a small donkey. If they were creatures of God they were, by definition, his brothers and sisters. Water was a sister and fire a brother. The flowers of the fields, the grass, the trees, earthworms, all were brothers and sisters. No stem could be cut off, no insect crushed without a warning word from Francis. Even putting out a fire could be a criminal act. "No, dearest brother, don't harm the fire," he said one day to a friar who had run to his aid because his tunic was burning. On another occasion Francis beseeched Brother Fire to be good to him when, in the last years of his life, the surgeon opened the veins between his ears and his eyebrows with a red-hot iron in an attempt to cure him of his eye ailment.

THE FINAL SEAL

Dante in Il Paradiso (*XI, 106*) *described in epic style the most extraordinary event in the Saint's life, when . . . "on the harsh rock between Tiber and Arno / from Christ did he receive that final imprint / which his limbs two years carried." In the 18th-century print reproduced here, the engraver emphasizes the steep cliff on the summit of which the miracle occurred; in the canvas of the Assisian painter Dono Doni, reproduced on the adjoining page and preserved today in the Pinacoteca of Assisi, the emphasis is dramatic and spiritual.*

Mount Verna was the last lap: Francis was drawn there by a mysterious presentiment. He arrived there on the back of a donkey because he could no longer walk on foot and was met by Count Orlando. About a year before, the Count had given him this spur of the mountain and now he wished to make the stay of the Saint and his three companions—Friar Leo, Friar Masseo, Friar Angelo—as comfortable as possible. The welcome was made even more festive by a multitude of birds who flew around him, chirping gaily. His biographers have minutely described the most important episode in the life of the *Poverello*, namely the Stigmata that made him similar to Christ.

A hut made of branches was built under a beech tree and Francis beseeched Friar Leo to keep everyone away from that place. He spent the Feast of the Assumption there, and penetrated further into the forest toward the cleft of the mountain. Friar Leo's task was to bring him a little bread and water once a day. In that solitude Francis relived the moments of the Passion of Jesus with such an intensity of love that he brought them to a vivid reality in his soul and upon his body. "While he was in a state of ecstasy with God one morning, as he was praying on a slope of the mountain, lo, he beheld a seraph with six wings resplendent with fire, descend from the heights of Heaven. When with his exceedingly swift flight he arrived in the air at a point near the man of God, the image of a crucified man appeared behind the wings. Two wings rose above the head, two others were spread as though poised in flight, and the last two entirely hid the body. At the sight of the vision, the servant of Christ was struck with a sense of wonderment and his heart was suffused with a joy mixed with pain . . . Upon disappearing, the vision left a prodigious ardor in his heart and imprinted upon his flesh marks no less prodigious. Indeed, soon thereafter the signs of nails, as he had seen them an instant before on that image of the crucified man, began to appear on his hands and feet. On his right side, he had the red scar of a wound as though he had been pierced by a lance." On that day, September 14, 1224, the sanctity of the Poor Man of Assisi was finally sealed.

"BROTHER BODY" IS WORN OUT

The 15th-century canvas in the hermitage of Greccio, reproduced here, shows Francis drying his eyes which teared constantly because of his eye disease. The painting is considered a copy of another which was commissioned, according to tradition, by the Roman noblewoman, Jacqueline of Settesoli, during the Saint's last years.

THE MYSTICAL FLIGHT OF THE SKYLARKS

Francis arrived at Porziuncola almost on the point of death; in the cell that was to receive his last breath, he asked all the friars to assemble around him "and placing his right hand on each one of them he blessed all those present and those absent and those who would join the Order in the future until the end of time." He blessed his successor, Friar Elias, with particular benevolence.

Then he anxiously awaited the arrival of Lady Jacqueline of Settesoli, the Roman noblewoman who is considered the mother of the Franciscan Third Order (the order of lay people). He had already sent his farewell to Clare and to other sisters with a stanza of verse. After being told that Francis was on the verge of death, Lady Jacqueline brought with her the ash-colored shroud for the burial, the candles, and the almond cakes of which he was so fond since in a dream she had been told of the dying man's desire for these sweets. Francis smiled at her from his pallet, tasted the sweets and blessed her.

Only one final greeting remained to be delivered now, the one to his beloved bride, Lady Poverty. He celebrated it with a rite. He had himself stretched out naked on the ground and ordered the attendant friars to gird him with the hairshirt and to spread ashes over him. And while they tried to restrain their tears, he said to them: "I have accomplished my work. May Christ teach you yours." He died on the evening of October 3, 1226, intoning with a thin voice a versicle from a psalm: "Free my soul from prison, so that I may praise Thy name." At that very instant a flock of skylarks rose above the roof, as though to accompany the soul of the Saint on his last journey.

The pictorial cycle by Benozzo Gozzoli in Montefalco concludes with this fresco of the burial rites of the Saint. A spectator who saw the Poverello composed in eternal slumber described him as follows: "His flesh, at first brown, now was resplendently white, and the limbs seemed to have acquired the sweetness and softness of an innocent babe's."

These two pages contain the series of frescoes, long attributed to Giotto, painted between 1315 and 1316 by the so-called Maestro delle Vele in the Basilica of Assisi. Above: the allegory of Franciscan poverty. "Show me, O Lord, the path of thy most delightful poverty," Francis used to say. "Poverty triumphs over all, she is queen of all. I languish for love of her, nor do I have rest without her." Maestro delle Vele also painted a fresco depicting an allegory

of obedience (below, left) and chastity (above). "He who gives himself in obedience entirely into the hands of the Superior renounces his body and his spirit," asserted the Saint. In defense of chastity, he said: "I firmly command all friars not to engage in any familiar or suspect talks with women." To crown the three Franciscan virtues, the unknown painter portrayed the Saint in glory being borne heavenward by a choir of fifty-three angels.

The precious relics of the
Saint, devoutly preserved in
Franciscan convents
to our day and
reproduced here, are
perhaps the most significant
ones. From left to right
and from top to bottom:
the beautiful processional
Romanesque cross,
which probably preceded
the funeral procession.
The chalice and the paten
used by St. Francis for
purification after Communion.
The chamois leather
which served to protect
the wound on the Saint's rib.
The pillow, embroidered
in gold, on which the
head of the Poverello of Assisi
rested after his death.

The Franciscan movement flourished mightily. The Friars Minor already numbered several thousand at the death of St. Francis. Towards the end of the 13th century the figure rose to 25,000. According to statistics gathered in 1316 there were 30,000 friars with 1400 convents. Even in our time, when poverty hardly seems to be a shining ideal, the Franciscans alone represent one-fifth of the great monastic army of the Church: 45,000 members out of 250,000. At present Franciscan friars are divided into three great families: the Friars Minor, the Conventual Friars Minor, and the Capuchin Friars Minor. The first wear a chestnut-colored habit, girded by a white rope, with the cowl hanging from a short cape. They wear sandals and do not use a hat. The Conventuals wear a black tunic, girded by a white string, with black cape and cowl. They wear shoes and hats. The Capuchins can be distinguished by their beards, prescribed by regulation. They wear a chestnut-colored habit, with a long and pointed cowl; sandals but no hats. Despite these external dissimilarities, the Franciscan friars live according to the same Rule, that which was dictated by St. Francis and which is inspired by the unchanging ideals of evangelical poverty, purity, humility and gladness.

1182—born in Assisi, son of Pietro Bernardone and Giovanna, called Pica.

1190-1195—attends school at the church of St. George.

1195-1200 spends his youth in pleasure haunts.

1201-1202—takes part in the struggle between Assisi and Perugia and fights in the battle of Collestrada where he is taken prisoner.

1203—November: released from prison and returns to the gay and carefree life as before. But he undergoes a psychological change.

1204—struck down by a serious illness he feels disgust for his empty life.

1205—he tries to give a purpose to his life by arming himself as a knight, and sets out for Apulia to enlist in the army of Gualtieri of Brienne.

1205—becomes ill in Spoleto and has a vision that marks the beginning of his conversion.

1205—returns to Assisi, gathers his old friends around him, but derives no pleasure from their feasts, only disillusion. Seeks solitude. Now converted, he goes on a pilgrimage to Rome. Arriving at St. Peter's, he dresses in rags and joins the beggars.

1206—in meditation in the tiny church of St. Damian on the slopes of Mount Subasio, he hears the voice of the Crucifix on the altar, which asks him to rebuild the church. In October, Pietro Bernardone has his son summoned before the magistrates to demand restitution of the money spent in the restoration of St. Damian. Francis appeals to Guido, bishop of Assisi, and publicly renounces his hereditary rights.

1207-1209—now dedicated to a life of prayer and solitude, he helps lepers and restores the churches of the area.

1209—he establishes himself in the chapel of St. Mary of the Angels and here, one day during the Mass, he hears a passage from the Gospel in which Christ outlines their mission to the apostles and thereby he has a revelation of what his task is to be. The very words of Christ are his first Rule.

1209-1210—the first followers join him who eventually will number twelve, excluding Francis. April 16, 1209 is considered the founding date of the Order.

1209-1210—Francis composes the first regulations of religious life.

1210—the Franciscan movement begins to spread in the adjoining regions with some opposition. Francis considers it opportune to ask for the approval of his Rule from the Pope. He goes to Rome with eleven friends. He is received by Innocent III and the latter verbally approves the Rule. Thus the Order achieves legal status.

1211—after the return from Rome the friars live first in Rivotorto and then in Porziuncola, but they move about in order to preach. They take the name of Friars Minor.

1212—Clare of Assisi, stirred by Francis' words, enters into religious life after a long preparation, giving rise to the Second Order. Francis, now dedicating himself to preaching, decides to go to the East. He sails for Palestine but contrary winds return him to Ancona.

1213—May 8: Count Orlando offers him Mount Verna as a gift.

1213-1214—leaves for Morocco, passing through France and Spain, but he is forced to return to Italy after he is struck by a serious illness before reaching his destination.

1215—meeting of the first General Chapter of Pentecost.

1216—July 16: Innocent III dies and is succeeded by Honorius III.

1219-1220—sails again for the Orient. Preaches before the Sultan of Egypt. Returns to Italy upon being notified of the crisis in the Order, due to the conflicts between the "laxists" and the "spirituals."

1221—the famous Chapter of the Mats is held.

1222—the apostolic journeyings continue. Towards the end of this year, he is worn out by his labors, and retires to the hermitage of Fonte Colombo, near Rieti.

1223—he prepares the Second Rule at Fonte Colombo and in October of that year he obtains sanction for it from Honorius III in the bull *Solet annuere* of November 29. On Christmas night of that year he celebrates the birth of Jesus in Greccio, setting up the first crib.

1224—after retiring in penance and mortification to Mount Verna, he suffers the Stigmata on September 14.

1225—gravely ill with an eye ailment and suffering from the Stigmata, he goes to Rieti to be medically treated at the papal court, but with no improvement.

1226—he spends the winter in Siena but when his illness worsens he is taken to Assisi where he composes the *Canticle of Creatures*. Sensing the end is near, he asks to be taken to Porziuncola. Exhausted, he dies between October 3 and 4 surrounded by his friars who, in accordance with his wishes, have placed him naked on the ground. The mortal remains are taken to the church of St. George in Assisi. Four years later, in 1230, they will be interred in the new Basilica named after him.

The works reproduced in this book are preserved in the following collections: in Assisi: Archive of the Basilica: p. 69; Lower Basilica: pp. 14, 39, 72, 73; Upper Basilica: pp. 18, 58; church of Rivotorto: pp. 24-25, 30, 66, 66-67; Museum of the Cathedral: pp. 6, 8-9, 39, 74; Palace of the Commune: p. 52; Sacristy of the Basilica: p. 55; San Damiano: pp. 18, 19, 25; St. Clare: pp. 40, 41, 42, 43; Santa Maria degli Angeli: pp. 21, 24, 32, 33 34, 39, 46, 47, 52-53, 53, 55, 56. Berlin, Staatsbibliothek: p. 15. Florence, Santa Croce: p. 55. Greccio: p. 64. Montefalco, St. Francis: pp. 4, 13, 16-17, 20-21, 28, 28-29, 36, 47, 49, 57, 60, 70. Rome: Biblioteca Casanatense: p. 65; Vatican Museum: p. 26; Museum of the Capuchins: pp. 17, 37, 47, 53, 60, 63, 68; St. Francis at Ripa: frontispiece. Siena, Palazzo Pubblico: pp. 10-11, 12. Subiaco, lower church: p. 38. Photographic credits: Alinari: frontispiece, pp. 27, 38, 39. Mondadori Photographic Archive: pp. 4, 7, 11, 15, 67. Vatican Photographic Archive: p. 26. Marzari: pp. 18, 58, 72, 73. Panicucci: credits. Agostino Ghilardi and Sergio Cerasoli were the editors responsible for the collection and execution of all the other illustrations.